SOLILOQUY OF 1971:

A MEMOIR OF THE LIBERATION WAR OF BANGLADESH

Soliloquy of 1971

A Memoir of the Liberation War of Bangladesh

REZAUL ISLAM

Soliloquy of 1971: A Memoir of the Liberation War of Bangladesh

By Rezaul Islam

Translated from the Bengali by the author. Bengali title: "একাত্তরের স্যালিলিয়াক্যুই" (Ekattorer Soliloquy).

English translation edited, skillfully and carefully, by Cordelia Fuller.

Cover art by M M Maksud Biplob, Architect.

Table of Contents

Foreword

Bangladesh's war of independence from Pakistan began in early 1971, and ended in December of that year. Rezaul Islam was a teenager during that period. This memoir describes his family's experiences in that tumultuous time. A sensitive and skilled writer in his native language (Bengali/Bangla), he published the original version of this book some years ago.

In the book, he also describes his encounters with young men who volunteered to make risky, secret journeys to India to be trained as fighters for their country's freedom, and then returned to take on the military government dominating their country.

CHAPTER 1: **FEBRUARY**

In mid-February, the sun had begun to rise a little earlier. When, at the end of the night, I looked at the sky, and saw that the brightness of the stars was beginning to dim, I knew it would soon be dawn. In the early morning, one by one, people wearing saris and Punjabi suits began to gather in front of the house. When twelve or thirteen people were gathered there, they began to sing, accompanied by a harmonium, and march along the Green Road[1] towards the Shaheed Minar. Apart from their singing, the road was silent. They sang, "Can I ever forget the 21st of February, that was stained with the blood of our brothers?" When this group reached the Science Laboratory, it was joined by a number of other groups. Then they all proceeded, together, through the New Market, to the Azimpur graveyard. Once they had paid tribute to Abdus Salam and Abul Barkat, they moved on to Salimullah Hall, crossing Plassey Road. Soon, this group found itself lost in the massive crowd gathered at Shaheed Minar. The ceremony ended with an homage to all of the martyrs, including Salam and Barkat, who were killed in 1952 for defending Bengalis' right to use their native language. It was for them that the Shaheed Minar had been constructed.

By the end of February, mounting political unrest had led to great turbulence, in Dhaka and

---

[1] Green Road is a road, and the name of a residential area, in Dhaka City.

around the country. There had been strong public excitement among Bengalis, after the all-Pakistan elections the previous December, when the mainly East Pakistan-based Awami League had won a landslide victory. But there were signs that the Pakistani military government was not going to respect the outcome of that election, and this led to great unrest among Bengalis. With East Bengal in this perturbed situation, my father, on February 26th, went to Chittagong on an emergency job. He was supposed to come back the next day. But he did not. Everybody in our house got worried. Telephone communications were very weak. We couldn't get any information about him. Two days later, however, he did finally return, looking very tired. Asked about the delay, he said, "Conditions in Chittagong are not good. There are continuous clashes between the Biharis[2] and the Bengalis. The army is supporting the Biharis. We have to be careful."

He told us that the train he boarded when he was first trying to return home had been stopped by furious mobs near Comilla. He eventually got to Dhaka, but only by changing buses many times, to make his way around all the troubles. Having seen the deterioration of conditions in Chittagong, he had known intuitively that the country as a whole would be in very bad shape, and that the Pakistani military government was not about to hand over power. As he told us this story, we wondered,

---

[2] "Biharis" are Urdu-speaking Muslim immigrants from non-Bengali states in India.

"Why won't the Pakistani government hand over power, after our great victories in the elections?!"

Bengalis had united behind their party, and after the election, celebrated the victory joyfully, claiming autonomy for Bengali East Pakistan. The victorious Awami League should have been able to form a government then. The people could not accept the military junta's excuses for not handing over power, and grew impatient. Dhaka became a city of protest marches. Many died in clashes between Bengalis and Biharis. A curfew was issued, but the regime still could not establish order in the country. The Bengalis did not leave the locations of their protests and demonstrations. Eastern Bengal had become a breeding ground for violence.

Even the sport of cricket became involved in these national troubles. In late February, a cricket match began, at Dhaka Stadium, between the Pakistan Cricket Control Board and Commonwealth XI. My younger brother and I would go to the stadium in the morning, with a group of friends from our neighborhood. We would return home in the afternoon, after watching the game. On the final day of the match, on the first of March, four or five young men unexpectedly entered the stadium, excitedly directing comments to the umpires, and gesticulating. Two of them pointed at the spectators, shouting loudly that they should come out onto the field. The spectators could not understand why these young men were doing this, and were unhappy that the game had thus been halted suddenly. A while later, three or four other young men also entered the stadium, and then actually did go onto the field, and the game had to be halted again. We were very unhappy about the game's being interrupted in this manner. When we came out of the stadium around midday, I saw that all the shops in the area – both in Gulistan and around Baitul Mukarram[3] - were closed. Bus, car and taxi services were not running. Thousands of people were on the streets, chanting slogans - *Joy Bangla, Joy Bangla!* [4] – Victory to the Bengali nation! There were demonstrators and protestors everywhere. We all soon learned that the inaugural meeting of the National Assembly, that had been scheduled for 3d March, had been postponed indefinitely by the Pakistani military junta. Hearing this news had made many Bengalis furious.

We now began walking towards home with our friends. On our way, we spotted Sheikh Mujibur Rahman (popularly known as Bangobandhu) and his aides, riding in the direction of Motijheel, or Gulistan, in a car. When we got home in the evening, Father scolded us for being late, but also asked us about what we had seen. We narrated everything in detail. When night came, we heard the news that Bangobandhu had, in a speech at

---

[3] Gulistan is a central area of Dhaka. Baitul Mukarram is the country's largest mosque, and is located very close to Gulistan.
[4] "Joy Bangla," loosely translated, means, "Victory to the Bengali nation"

Purbani Hotel, declared the start of a non-cooperation movement against the Pakistani junta.

CHAPTER 2: MARCH

The non-cooperation movement began in the first week of March, when it became known that the inaugural meeting of the National Assembly would not be held. Dhaka was paralyzed. All of the schools, colleges, offices, mills, and factories were closed. Having this break from school, young people like me remained in holiday mood. Meanwhile, rumors and speculation were running wild in our house. Some of Father's friends from the neighborhood would come over, and pass the time discussing various issues. They would say things like, "This time the Bengalis have to get power! Power belongs to The People!!" "A successful transfer of power will happen through the non-cooperation movement!" We, the young people standing nearby, listened raptly to these declarations. Soon we heard that Bangobandhu Sheikh Mujibur Rahman was going to give a speech on 7th March, and we began, excitedly, to make preparations to attend it. Everyone was eager to hear what Bangobandhu would say. Masses of people flocked to the Race Course Ground on 7th March.

My uncle, Father's younger brother, who had been elected as a Member of the National Assembly (MNA), representing Sailkupa, in 1970, sent his jeep for us at noon, and immediately the jeep filled up, and left for the Race Course Ground. However, once the jeep reached Nilkhet, it got stuck, and could move no further. Crowds of people were marching on the streets, and shouting slogans. Thousands of them marched on toward the Race Course Ground. We got out of the jeep and joined the crowds. The Race Course Ground was then a horse-racing ground. There was a wooden fence encircling it. Everyone rushed to the fence, and then crossed it, and then waited eagerly to hear the speech. Then the dramatic moment arrived. Our Great leader, Sheikh Mujibur Rahman, began his speech. As his speech continued, the level of excitement in the massive crowd seemed to reach a fever pitch. Those unable to stand close to the speaker could not bear the passion of the moment. His audience listened intently, as if they were drinking in his words. When the leader directed them to, the people would raise high the four-foot-long bamboo poles that many of them carried, and chant the slogan, *Joy Bangla*. It seemed as if all of the people had become freedom fighters, and as if all Bengalis were infused with a great spirit of enthusiasm. We felt as if we were on a great journey from darkness to light.

After March 7, a firm conviction and determination to oppose the Pakistani oppressors developed in the people. Our flag displayed a map of Bangladesh on a red circle, on a green field. One day, when I was walking around the neighborhood with a close friend of the family, we met a retired soldier, who told us that he had begun training himself up for combat again, at night. Secret discussions were going on, he said, regarding resistance, and ways to prevent the Pakistan Army from entering the locality. He advised that empty big drums, blocks of wood, and bricks should be set out on our street. We busied ourselves with obtaining these items and arranging them according to his instructions, and other related activities. Our interest in, and excitement about, the resistance, grew from this kind of participation. By this time, Bangobandhu had started negotiations with Pakistani President Yahya Khan. At one point, Zulfikar Ali Bhutto, whose party had won a majority of the parliamentary seats in West Pakistan in 1970, also joined the talks. Every day it seemed as if a settlement was closer to being achieved. But that didn't happen. The talks continued for some time. The hopes of the Bengali people rose and fell, and rose and fell again. Who could know what the future held?

I was in grade 12. Every morning I used to leave Green Road, with three or four other boys from the neighborhood, and head to Ramna Park, by way of the Science Laboratory. Then we would return to our neighborhood, passing by the Sakura Restaurant, which was opposite the Inter-Continental Hotel. We would also pass through Hatirpool and Kanthalbagan on the way home. On 25th March, during this trip, we made a stop, as we often did, at the Office of *The People's Newspaper*, which was near the Sakura Restaurant. The first page of the paper was mounted on the wall, displaying a picture of Mr. Bhutto viewing Dhaka City using a telescope. It showed the city as flooded with Bangladesh flags. In the picture, it looked as if East Pakistan was no more. The picture alarmed us, making us wonder what the Pakistan army had been up to. Nevertheless, we went to play cricket at the Dhanmondi Cricket

Ground, which was just beyond Staff Quarters, the government officers' housing complex. We soon got absorbed in our Cricket game. But suddenly a middle-aged man appeared and told us, "Boys, you should go home now. Things are looking bad." We stopped the game and headed home, walking past the Staff Quarters. It was evening, and few cars were on the road. The city seemed excessively quiet, and gloomy.

Darkness holds mysteries. I fell asleep that night, but then, after midnight, I awoke to hear my parents whispering. I thought, at first, that I saw lightning flashing. But the sky was unclouded. I heard terrible sounds of shooting. Was Dhaka City to be destroyed like Hiroshima and Nagasaki? Father and Mother seemed very worried. Their anxiety also made the rest of us nervous. The Pakistan army had deployed tanks, bombs, and machine guns against the Bengali people. How many innocent creatures were going to die on that night of 25th March, 1971? It was a terrible night. No one who had not witnessed it would be able to believe it had happened! There were massacres throughout the country, and thousands of innocent people were killed that night. And then a curfew was imposed, for an indefinite period.

Two days later, the curfew was relaxed for a few hours in the morning. So then, Father sent me to visit his youngest brother, whom we called Kuti[5] Uncle . I got on the bus at the Staff Quarters bus stand. While we were passing Jagannath Hall,

---

[5] "Kuti" means "youngest".

which was spotted with bullet holes, I heard a Bihari man, who was sitting near a window, burst out laughing and remark sarcastically, "What's happened now? The hounds have been gunned down!" It upset me terribly to hear this horrible joke about the army's killing of so many of our people.

When the bus reached the area of the Medical Hospital, I got off, and walked through the university campus to Kuti Uncle's house. It seemed as if the world was ending. Our people's dreams had been shattered. What was the point of all of Sheikh Mujib's actions and speeches now? What would become of us? Life had been better before the election. Now it seemed that we would become the slaves of the Biharis. Kuti Uncle was a university professor. I told him about what I had seen and heard on the bus. He counseled me, "As the situation is right now, it seems like it's better not to talk about such things. But maybe conditions will improve."

After 25th March, Dhaka was like a ghost town. At night, it was as if the silence of the grave had descended upon us. Our lively city was no more. Every evening the Army, to further alarm people, would set fire to tires, trees, bushes, and other things. The city's anxious residents passed their nights quietly. Lights were turned off in most homes at night. We heard the sounds of automobiles in the quiet night. The barking of the local dogs added to the ghostly atmosphere. Now Father would become very restless, and walk around his room, sometimes turning on the radio, and waiting to hear something. It seemed that our people's efforts had been in vain, that there was no more hope for us, no future ahead. Our radio was a big one, and not working well; it produced loud static when turned on. The loud noise spoiled our efforts to stay quiet, for the sake of security, frightening my mother, who snapped at Father, "You will die, and you will allow all of us to die." Father listened to her, but he could not calm down and be still. Suddenly one night, he heard a faint human voice amid the static, echoing Bangobandhu's calls for the liberation of the Bengali people.

People had been saying, during the non-cooperation movement, that the power of the people united would be invincible. "The people's power is stronger than that of the atomic bomb," they said. But after the savage attacks on civilians of 25th March took place, the resistance collapsed like a house of cards. Since the military crackdown, the people had been feeling hopeless. Then, one night, my MNA uncle arrived quietly at our house. His face looked very serious. He was wearing a churidar pajama, and his beard was shabby. Seeing him like this alarmed us. As he entered the house, he said to Father, "It is not safe to remain in Dhaka. Everyone else has fled. Not a single one of those elected to parliament is in the capital. The army is looking to capture all of us. I have to flee. I will stay here tonight, and leave tomorrow." Father frowned with concern, but tried to reassure him, "It will be all right, don't worry."

The MNA uncle passed the night in our house, pacing the floor. Then, the next day, he left. We worried that he might not be able to get to his destination safely.

Towards the end of March, we began to hear rumors that the Pakistani military had started kidnapping young men in the dead of night, and then torturing them. Father and Mother now became extremely anxious. Within a day, a report came that two or three boys had been taken from Kalabagan, a neighborhood very close to us. Rumors were rampant. And why not? Rumors were our news. When people are confined to their homes, and cannot easily get access to reliable news, rumors will multiply. But we knew that this rumor was probably not accurate. The original source of the information was unknown. But then, a little later, we suddenly heard that the two eldest sons of a Customs Officer had disappeared. Nobody could say where they had gone. We knew that this story was not just a rumor. Such things were really happening. Young men were being abducted, and taken to the cantonment. Those who had talked about guerrilla warfare during the non-cooperation movement were targeted - those who had seemed to be leaders. Those two missing brothers had been offering advice about guerrilla warfare to people in our neighborhood. Both had been brilliant students. One of them had achieved amazing results at the Science Laboratory School. He was also very handsome. The news of the disappearances terrorized our parents. My mother's brother, too, was involved in politics. And our house was a hotbed of political discussion; so we thought it would be a major target. For his wife and children to be safe, Father thought, we needed to go away somewhere, anywhere. Then, a cousin of Father's, whom we called "Ranga Uncle[6]," came running over to our house. He lived in Dhaka's Rayer Bazar neighborhood. He was an officer of the East Pakistan Small Industries Corporation.

He told Father, "It is not safe to be here in Dhaka. Let your family come with my family to the house in the village." Father questioned him, "But how will you get there? It's not easy to get transport out there. That house is far away from Dhaka.

The uncle responded, "I will arrange for a boat. It may take some time for us to get there, but we must go."

Two or three days later, we left for the village house. Ranga Uncle came by to pick us up. We were very reluctant to go, and leave Father almost alone at home.

All of our things were in the house we were leaving. We were uncertain about how we would travel. We were unhappy about the whole thing. Still, we had to go. As we left home, we were saddened to see Father standing alone in front of the house, bidding farewell to us. He wasn't saying anything, as he had nothing more to say! Rashid, the young man whom we called "Brother," who

---

[6] The word "ranga" is used to describe the color of a white person's skin, although it can also mean "reddish" or "colored".

had moved in with us as a teenager, after his parents died, and who used to assist with various chores around the house, went to join Father there, rubbing his tearful, swollen eyes with a towel.

On about 28th March, my mother, elder sister, and brothers and I got on three rickshaws and set off for Ranga Uncle's house in Rayer Bazar. We rode there through empty streets. Luckily, we did not come across any Pakistani soldiers on our way. The neighborhood, which had formerly been predominantly Hindu, was now almost deserted; we knew that this was because Hindus had been fleeing from the city for their lives; we didn't know where they had gone. After we got to Ranga Uncle's house, another man arrived there and declared, 'We're going to go to Basila village. Basila lies across a narrow stream from Rayer Bazar, and stands on the Buriganga River. We'll try to get a boat on the river from there."

We began to walk towards Basila. Several branches of the Buriganga river meet in that area, as it is at a very low elevation. The only way for us to get there was by walking across a rough field. There were large chunks of soil scattered all around. The walking was very difficult. In the month of March there generally is no water in the stream that lies between Rayer Bazar and Basila. So we could not take a boat to Basila. Eventually we reached Basila, a small village on the Buriganga river. There was no light there, no electricity. We were upset to discover this, especially when we thought about Father's having been left almost alone in the Dhaka house. The man who had taken us to the village invited us up into his house. He was a milkman, who had long supplied Ranga Uncle's house with milk. He and his family went to stay at the house of some nearby friends, to make room for us. We settled in his tiny house. There was no boat available in the area for the next few days. We had no idea how long we would have to wait. We could not eat, sleep, or bathe properly there. We were frustrated.

1st April, night. We lay down on the mud floor of the house, and began to wait for sleep. I heard the rumble of a launch coming from the south, on the river, and remarked on it. Suddenly we were all wide awake, and jumped up to go outside and look around. We could see that there was a search light shining from the launch. This frightened us badly. However, after a while the launch moved on, and we relaxed a bit, and went inside to lie down again, falling into a deep sleep. But early the next morning, we were awoken by the sounds of heavy gunfire. It seemed that Doomsday was coming for the little village. People were running, screaming, and crying. A loud megaphone voice advised, "Go down through the west side of the village and run off somewhere, anywhere, before the Army comes into the village. Quickly, quickly, please."

We were very scared. People did not know where they were going, but just dispersed, running aimlessly. After a little while, I saw my elder sister standing alone near the village mosque. She was adjusting a sari that she had put on, to look like an ordinary rural woman. She was hoping, desperately, to find safety in the mosque. It was very upsetting to me to see her like this. We were all so helpless! I told her to wait there for a bit, for me to go fetch Mother and Auntie (Ranga Uncle's wife). But as I began talking to those women, I heard Ranga Uncle announce, "We'll all go together. Don't be afraid of them. May Allah bless us all." The milkman's house was now empty.

We all followed Ranga Uncle. Thousands of frightened people were now gathered on a big patch of rough field in Basila. What actions human survival instincts will drive us to perform! We were all running, but to unknown destinations. Someone in the family had a big trunk, that our group tried to carry cooperatively. I had it on my shoulder for a while, and then my younger brother and I carried it together for a while, each holding one of the handles at its ends. I worried that this might break our arms. Then, suddenly, there was a helicopter in the sky, apparently coming after us. It circled over our heads several times. This frightened us badly, and we tried to run faster. Sometimes we fell down on the rough road, and then got ourselves up again, to continue running. It was as if we were on a battleground. Then, by chance, we met a friend of a maternal uncle of mine. He was very surprised to see us. He asked, "What are you doing here?"

I said, "We had fled from Dhaka. Now we are attempting to go back to Dhaka. The army has been chasing us. I don't know if we'll be able to get to Dhaka." The uncle's friend said, "A lot of the people who've left Dhaka are have been joining the resistance. They are now being assaulted by the army. The army attacked Jinjira union.[7] There were some people there who had joined together to fight the army. That's why this operation was started. I've heard that many people were killed in Jinjira. The army burnt down most of the houses in the villages. "

I asked him, "Aren't you in the army?"

He responded sharply, "Shut your mouth, please! Someone else might hear. I've escaped. I cannot return to Dhaka. I will have to hide here and hide there. You cannot keep on carrying that trunk. Give it to me. Let me carry it for a while."

After walking with us for a while, he said, "I cannot go any further. You're going back to Dhaka. Keep going. Stay well. I'll see you again sometime."

He went off in another direction. We were looking forward to getting to the house in Dhaka, but first we had to get to Rayer Bazar. This was not easy. We arrived there at about 11 am. Then Ranga Uncle called for a rickshaw, and sent us home to Green Road. Once again, the streets were practically empty. I was nervous, worrying that we might run into the army, but that didn't happen. When we got close to home, we saw Father, standing with a group of people in front of a neighbor's house, chatting with them. Then he also saw us, and was surprised, and rushed out to us.

---

[7] In Pakistan and Bangladesh, a "union" is a local, rural, administrative unit consisting of several villages.

There were signs of happiness, as well as nervousness, on his face.

He said, "What is this? Why are you looking so devastated?"

Mother said, "It is only by the grace of Allah that we are still alive."

Father, having a good idea of what she might be talking about, exclaimed, "Enough of fleeing here and there! Whether we live or die, let's all do it together."

We happily reassembled our family at home. Birds were flying free in the blue sky. There was sweet sunshine on the rooftop of our house. The trees stood there peacefully.

I took comfort in these aspects of nature, happy to see that they had remained constant. It was only the people living with that nature that had changed. The thought flashed through my mind that there was now no peace, no delight, no happiness in the life of the people who resided in this land.

That night, Father opened up his diary, and began to try to read something to us from it, but stopped. Instead, his voice trembling with emotion, he said, "When you were not here, I used to write in this book on my lonely, melancholy nights, hoping you would read it after my death." Later, he tore up the pages of the diary. We saw tears in the eyes of this brave man who we had believed to be as strong and immovable as a rock.

Now there was steadiness in Dhaka city life. The disturbances had ceased, and there was also no busy-ness. The schools, colleges, and offices still had not opened. During the day, a few people used to come to our house and talk about the future of the country. Everyone feared the worst for it. A friend of Father's used to come over. This friend, who had been so vocal during the non-cooperation movement, had now become nearly silent. He talked about hoping that India would recognize Bangladesh. His remarks provoked sharp comments from Father. "Yes, how long will it take them to recognize our country?" he said. "If we die, will they do it then? How is it that even the conscience of the World, the United Nations, cannot do anything? Why are they all so silent now? Is there no humanity left in this world? Thousands of people are dying daily. But the world is silent!"

Thus did Father express his severe disappointment with the failure of the United Nations to support the Bengali struggle.

CHAPTER 3: **APRIL**

On most days, I would go to the market – but not by walking along the road, where vehicles full of hostile and aggressive Pakistani soldiers were likely to be encountered. Instead, I would take a short cut, climbing over the wall at the back of our house, and jumping down into a narrow lane that led to the market.

The market, although it did open, was not in full swing. There was no fish to be had there, and no vegetables. Most of the stalls were closed. Almost everybody had disappeared. After buying rice, potatoes, eggs, and lentils, I would return home. Day after day, those were the only things we had to eat.

My father would turn on the radio at night. We used to listen to Kolkata Radio for the news, with the volume lowered to a whisper. One day, it was reported that the town of Kushtia had been liberated by freedom fighters in the area. We dared not trust this report, as my maternal grandparents' home was in Kushtia District. When my mother heard it, she exclaimed, "Ha! Can your uncles fight?" The next day, we actually saw Sabre Jets flying over our heads in Dhaka. And it wasn't only for one day. For the next two or three days, we kept seeing them. That implied that something had indeed happened. Many people were saying that Kushtia had been bombed by such planes. Now we knew that the report from Kolkata Radio had been correct.

Our house, which had been a lively, social place, had now become lifeless. No visitors came by. Father was not going to his office anymore, and my siblings and I were no longer going to school. We would all just stay at home, and eat our meals quietly; and late at night, we would listen to the radio. Then, one day, Ranga Uncle came over from his house in Rayer Bazar. He told my father, "Seraj, we're going to the village house. Now everything is alright over there. If you want to stay here and die, you can do it, but I will take your two older boys along with me." Ranga Uncle was adamant about this. Reluctantly, Father asked us to make preparations to go. My younger brother had an adventurous spirit, and hoped to join a group of freedom fighters out in the countryside. But my heart was against leaving the city. However, it seemed that I was now obliged to go. Bidding farewell to my mother, sisters, and littlest brother, I set out for the village with Ranga Uncle and my younger brother. As we were leaving, my father came down to advise us, 'If you get lost, then tell people, "We're going to Sailkupa. My father's name is Serajul Islam and my grandfather's name is Moulvi Shamsuddin Ahmed."' My father was reluctant to let us go, but he had given up on arguing with Ranga Uncle.

We went to Ranga Uncle's house in Rayer Bazar, and waited for him to tell us about the plans for the journey to the village. When a few hours had passed, and there were no signs, yet, of journey preparations, I said to my younger brother, "I don't want to go to the village. Let's go back home."

My brother said, "Why? There is a war going on in this country! We will take up guns, and fight them."

I told him, "If you want to fight, then you fight. I will go home."

He did not reply.

The next time Ranga Uncle came by us, I said to him, "Uncle, I do not feel good. I miss my mother. I am feeling pretty bad." He gazed at me for a long time. I think he could see my sadness in my face. He said, "OK, then go home. I'll call a rickshaw for you."

My younger brother and I went back home. Later, we heard that Ranga Uncle's family had left for the village that very night, by boat. We knew that it was only because Uncle loved us very much, that he had wanted to take us out to the village.

There was constant shooting in Dhaka. People were afraid, and they had begun to flee from Dhaka quietly, heading for their village homes. Two or three of the families in our Green Road neighborhood had left. Father, not being able, in a country full of danger, to keep in touch with our relatives, or to go to his office, was anxious and restless.

Then, one day, a friend of Father's, who was an engineer, and whom my siblings and I called Engineer Uncle (although his name was Badiuzzaman), came to the house. He said, "We have to leave Dhaka. Things are bad here, and they seem to just keep getting worse."

Father hesitated about whether to stay in Dhaka, or leave. After thinking about his closed office and the security of his family, he agreed to leave. So now, we would all finally be leaving Dhaka. After four or five days, we received word that a launch had been hired to take us to our family's village. It would pick us up at Narayanganj. We fixed the twentieth of April as our date for leaving. Our furniture was shifted over to a next-door neighbor's house. Our precious records of Tagore's songs were sent to Kuti Uncle's house.

Our taking these measures reminded me that, about a month ago, during the country's non-cooperation movement, we had sold our car at a very low price, and locked many of our other goods in one selected room in the house. I also remembered that, when my family had moved to Dhaka, when I was five or six years old, I had been completely fascinated by the city, taking close note of its details, such as the fact that the streets had lamp posts with gas lamps on them. I would watch in rapt attention as the municipality's lamplighter ignited our local street lamp, using his long pole. I would also gaze raptly at the porter who carried a leather bag filled with water around our neighborhood, selling the water to thirsty neighbors who were not receiving municipal water services in their homes. It was a matter of great sorrow and pain for me to leave this city that I had loved from my childhood. I really didn't want to leave Dhaka. It was also hard to be moving away from my friends. But the brutal reality was that we had to leave. The dire state of the city was forcing us to leave. On the afternoon of our departure, some of our neighbors gathered outside the house. Someone complained, "You're leaving us? It was giving us hope, until now, knowing that you were here."

We hired three Baby Taxis (small, three-wheeled vehicles) to take us to Narayanganj. I really couldn't bear to part from this beloved place. The taxis started off, but moved slowly. I looked back, and saw our neighbors standing in front of the house. I kept my eyes on them for as long as I could see them. "Who knows if we will ever meet again," I thought. They just stood there helplessly. They were out of sight by the time the baby taxis turned the corner.

We arrived in Narayanganj in the evening. That part of the trip had gone smoothly. We took a boat across the river, and got to Engineer Uncle's house. The house was already full of people. Engineer Uncle said to Father, "We were just talking about you, we were a bit worried. Traveling from Dhaka can be dangerous. However, you made it, you're here now. Now we don't need to worry. We will be leaving tomorrow morning. We have heard that an Army patrol boat will be here in two days. We have to leave before that. "

Father said, "Then we would be in danger. What will you do if they stop our launch?"

"Trust in Allah," said Engineer Uncle.

We passed an anxious night. We – seventeen members of three families – were all going to board a launch together. In the early morning, we saw our launch on the river Shitalakshya. The launch had a crew of four men.

It took off from the port of Narayanganj very quietly and cautiously. We were murmuring prayers to Allah, that He would keep us safe. There were no other launches, ships, or boats on the river. We knew we were risking death by sailing out on the Shitalakshya here, near Narayanganj. The expected army patrol boat could well come after us from behind. Eventually, our launch put some distance between us and Narayanganj. And once we found ourselves on the bigger, wider river – the Padma - having left the smaller river behind, our thoughts of death vanished.

Our launch encountered waves on the Padma, that splashed over us, but we kept on going. In the heat of noon, we longed to soak our bodies in the big river. It was a very wide river. We couldn't see its edge, or any other boats. The launch kept on moving throughout the day. Before sunset, it was docked at a village market. We spent the night there. Some lighthearted songs from Kolkata Radio could be heard from another boat. Despite the pain, sorrow and tension we had been experiencing, the songs cheered us, reminding us of the colorful and happy times we had had in our lives. Reminiscing about those earlier days, we went to sleep. The next day, around sunrise, we were awakened by the sound of the launch taking off again. The monotonous journey continued. The launch crossed over several branches of the great Padma that day. Behind the sand dunes along the riverbank, we could see paddy fields dancing gently, swaying in the wind. Nature was untroubled by our human concerns. So, the rice plants could sway and dance. But we humans could not dance like that. The days rolled on. One afternoon, the driver of the launch said, "Gopalganj Road, Takerhat, is ahead. We will purchase oil for the launch there. If you want to buy something there too, you can."

There were numerous people standing on the riverbank at Takerhat, chanting the slogan "Joy Bangla," when the launch arrived there. Our new green and red flag, with the golden map of Bangladesh on it, waved gently in the wind. They told us that Gopalganj had been liberated, and that Sheik Kamal, the son of Bangabandhu (Sheikh Mujibur Rahman), was trying to organize all the people in the region. Once our purchases of rice, lentils and oil had been made, the launch started off again. In the evening, we anchored safely on the riverbank. We spent a second night in the launch. Then, the next morning, we started our journey again. This journey had no pleasure to it. We just longed to know - when would we get to our village home?

Two days later, in the afternoon, the driver of the launch told us, "We have come near to Kamarkhali (a big market town). It is not very far - just four to five miles."

We were now traveling on the Madhumati river. It was four or five in the afternoon. But then, several of the people on the riverbank waved down the launch, saying we should stop it. The launch was slowly brought to a stop. The people standing on the riverbank told us, "It is not possible to move further. The Pakistani troops have occupied Kamarkhali. There has been heavy shooting. They have burnt down people's houses. Many people have died. You should go back."

So, once again it seemed that we were in great danger! Engineer Uncle asked my father, "What do we do now? Should we go back to Dhaka?" This was the big question – what to do. One of the people along the riverbank asked us, "Where do you want to go?"

Engineer Uncle said, "Sreepur".

The other man said, "Good, you'll be able to get there. We'll arrange for horse carts. Get off your boat now."

Our family got down from the launch. Four of our fellow passengers, who had been very close to us over the last three days, now bade farewell to us. They. As they were leaving, they held our hands, saying, "Brothers, pray for us. If we survive, we will see you again. "

Then the launch started up again, this time in the direction of the capital. It was evening, but not yet night time. In shadowy darkness, the launch moved away slowly. The local villagers had come forward spontaneously to assist us, and now they arranged for about ten horse carriages for us. This was not an easy thing to arrange. The villagers had stopped our launch before Kamarkhali, so that we could stay out of danger. Their helpfulness sincerely touched our hearts. Danger can bring people closer together. We got into one of our family's two carriages, and we all set off for Magura District.

One of the carriage drivers said he knew the road well. He would guide all the others. Our carriage was towards the back of the caravan. We could now feel that we were moving, but we could not see the road we were on. It was very dark. There was thunder and lightning in the sky.

Someone said he had heard that Magura town was being bombed by Pakistani troops – maybe the thunder was really the sound of bombing? Then, suddenly, it started raining. Water began to roll off the roof of the cart. The dry stalks of grain that we were sitting on soon got wet. It went on raining for a long time. We began to shiver with cold. The drivers of the horse carriages stopped them, and took shelter under them. Then, gradually, the rain stopped, and we started moving again, along a muddy, wet, road. The carriages now moved steadily for some time, but then, suddenly, stopped in an isolated place. There was no town or village nearby. It turned out that the leader coachman had forgotten the directions. Engineer Uncle was furious. He angrily shouted at the drivers, "Shout out loudly, to see if there is anyone nearby." One of them obediently called out, "Anyone there? Anyone there?"

A few moments later, a burly-looking man appeared in the nearby field, with a hurricane light in hand. Engineer Uncle told him that we wanted to go to the home of his relative Abul Ahsan, in Alokdia. "We have forgotten the way to Alokdia. Which way is it?"

The man with the hurricane light asked, "Pir Sahib's house?" (using a title for Abul Ahsan's father indicating that he was locally recognized as a spiritual leader).

Engineer Uncle said, "Yes."

The man with the light gave directions to the carriage drivers. We reached Abul Ahsan's house in Alokdia late that night. Our clothes were wet, and the cold had weakened us. We barely changed clothes before lying down on the simple beds in Abul Ahsan's one-room guesthouse. We had been very tired throughout the day, and the previous night. So we slept deeply.

The next morning, two horsemen, with carriages, came by. We bade farewell to Engineer Uncle and his relatives, and got into the carriages, which got us to our village home by mid-afternoon, driving along the wide canal roads. As we rode along in the noontime heat, we longed to dive into the canals, to cool down. In the first village we passed, all the small children were bathing in the canal water. The people around the canal stared curiously at us as we went by. We still had fifteen miles to travel to get to Katlagari, via Langolband. Once we finally entered our own village, we saw that the local kids had started following our horse carriages on foot, and we heard the elderly people exclaiming, "Well, who is arriving now?"

The horse carriage carrying me, my father, my younger brother, and Rashid stopped in front of the house's courtyard. One by one, we got down from the horse cart. Two cousin-brothers[8] of my father

---

[8] A "cousin-brother" is a male first cousin. Similarly, a "cousin-sister" is a female first cousin.

(both "Uncle" to me) came out, and welcomed us warmly. They seemed as pleased to see us, as if they had found a lost diamond. They seemed to adore us. We really had arrived in our ancestral home! After seven days of struggle and troubles, we were here! For a few moments, we forgot all the pain and tension of the past week. There is enormous joy in surviving danger!

When Father got down from the carriage, he said to one of the uncles, "Brother, our home looks just as I remember it. We were concerned about you when you left Dhaka. But now we are finally all home together. Where is our older brother?"

The uncle said, "He went to Mirzapur village with his family. They fled to that village when they heard that the army was coming here. But we didn't leave. What will be, will be, I say."

Father said, "I also won't leave. We have left Dhaka, where things are very bad. We've had plenty of hardship. After all that, where else would we go now?"

The neighbors assembled in our house and courtyard, and looked at us with curiosity. And why shouldn't they? We hadn't been to the village for more than a decade. When my paternal grandparents had lived in the village, after my grandfather's retirement from his government job, we used to come to the village when it was time for the Eid Festival. Eid in our childhood had been filled with joy and happiness. Father and the uncles would all gather together then. We, the little boy and girl cousins, would spend some merry days together. But, then, my grandparents left the village, and those joyous events came to an end. This time, it was our state of crisis that had brought us to the village. Although it had been so long since our last visit, the villagers made no complaints, but just welcomed us warmly. The village, which had been abstract and obscure to us for a long time, was now our host. We became very emotional now, as the villagers watched us eagerly.

The house was an old, wooden one, but it had not yet been damaged by insects. The tin roof had been red in color, but had now become pale with age. There was an open courtyard in front of the house. There was a pond near the courtyard. There were two mango trees by the front door. There was a well under one of the mango trees. There was a small local mosque, built of bricks, but with a tin roof and walls, directly to the west side of the house. There was a slice of land between the mosque and the house that was full of bush. There were some graves in the ground there, that were, some people said, the graves of our ancestors. Our family was placed in a corner room towards the back of the house. The villagers made the room clean and tidy for us. For as long as the situation in Dhaka did not improve, this room would be our home.

It felt like a new, more optimistic, day, but we could not watch the sunrise that would have seemed appropriate for it. When evening began to fall upon the village, I set out to walk around it, and happily found that it was full of thriving, dark green, leafy plants. I began conversations with some villagers who were to become, essentially, my village grandfather, uncle, and brothers -– as well as regular partners with us in our daily activities. Many of the current villagers had worked in more industrial places in the country, like Mongla port, or the sugar mill at Jagati, in Kushtia District. Some had worked in government offices. Now they had fled back home to this, their native village, out of fear for their lives. They dared not go back to their old jobs in the country's current deadly situation. They were concerned about their loss of income, but had felt they had no other choice than to come back here.

On most evenings in the village, its more prominent figures would assemble in our courtyard, and conduct their discussions, which would go on for a long time. My father and Ranga Uncle would sit on small stools. Many people would sit on mats. Others of us would stand nearby and listen. Auntie would serve us tea, without milk. It was sweetened with molasses, instead of sugar. We fully enjoyed drinking the tea despite all we had recently gone through. Father and Ranga Uncle told everyone the story of the atrocities of 25th March -- the night when about a million innocent Bengalis were brutally murdered by the Pakistan Army; and the story of the massacre of over a thousand at Jinjira; and that of our terror when we first tried to escape from Dhaka by launch, by way of Basila village, and of the subsequent escape of some members of our family from Basila village. Everyone was shocked to hear about these events. Many of the villagers exclaimed, "Muslims cannot do such things! And those people call themselves Muslims?"

Ranga Uncle replied, "What is a Muslim? Just like the British, what they want to do is to exploit others. They do not want to hand over power." We had grim thoughts about the country's future. Would all this sorrow and pain never end? The answer was not known. As the day went on, and the ground heated up under the sun, the local breezes grew hotter, so that the evening felt very hot. But, to the north of our house, the bamboo trees swayed, helping to cool us down some.

In early April, while we were still in Dhaka, the Pakistan Army had occupied Jessore and Jhenaidah. There had been pockets of resistance to Pakistani domination, scattered across the country, then. However, those efforts were weak, and short-lived, and not well-organized. People would try to resist as they could, but not in an organized way. We had stopped at Takerhat, near Faridpur, when we were coming to the village by launch. Takerhat had been freed then. But by the time we got there, the Pakistan Army had recaptured the city of Jhenaidah. Three of Father's brothers had been living in Jhenaidah before March. But Jhenaidah was now a practically uninhabited city. The two youngest brothers had fled to India by the time of the Pakistani re-occupation. And my father's oldest brother, who had been the Vice Principal of Jhenaidah Cadet College, had fled to our village with his family, also taking another family -- the family of the Principal -- with them. But, having heard that the Pakistan Army was coming to the village, he had left it, to take shelter in the neighboring village of Mirzapur. My father's immediate junior brother, the elected MNA, had escaped Dhaka after the atrocities of 25th March, to go to India, where he had joined the Provisional Government of Bangladesh, in its capital-in-exile in Kolkata. Meanwhile, his family had gone into hiding in the village of Tupipara, in Magura District.

Pakistani troops took control of the whole country within a few days. They set up camps at different Police Stations, and gradually consolidated their position. For strategic reasons, they would often drive around in jeeps, patrolling the villages. This scared people badly, and often led to panic. The army kept on terrorizing the nearly broken people of the villages. There was always fear. People often thought about leaving their villages, for fear of being captured and tortured by the army. By early May, taking shelter in others' villages had become a common thing. This seemed to be a sad, silent surrender, by too many of the people!

CHAPTER 4: **MAY**

April is supposed to be a month of rain and storms. There had been no rain in the beginning of April, and also none in the middle of the month. The sun kept glaring down on the village, and the soil remained very thirsty in the scorching heat. We could not sleep at night in the heat. In the early mornings, sometimes gentle breezes would soothe us a bit. During the day, people would try to stay under the shade of the trees, and to spend some time resting in their houses' outside rooms. In the evenings, as the sun's heat became less intense, people would find some relief.

My father's cousin, whom we called "Black Uncle" because he had a dark complexion, took on new work for us in the intense heat – that of planting brinjals[9] on the shore of the pond. Our days of idleness were over. He would come and call to us, to wake us up, early in the morning, so we could do our work before the sun brought the full heat of mid-day to the village. I would work with my younger brother and an elder cousin-brother named Ranzu, who was the son of my second-oldest uncle. We would dig up the soil with spades. The planting work continued every day for some weeks. Once that was done, we were given further work to do in the fields. We would provide food on the rice fields for the workers who worked there, during their work day, as a supplement to their wages.

---

[9] "Brinjals" are eggplants (or aubergines)

Some of our lands were cultivated by other families, who shared their crop with us. And some of our lands were cultivated by wage workers whom we would feed on the fields. After feeding them, I would go and sit in a solitary place, and look all around me, and at the sky. The fields looked infinitely wide to me from there. Memories of the few months I had spent as a college student – my golden days - flashed through my mind - when I would listen to music on Kolkata Radio, watch movies, play sports, and hang out with friends – when I was a kid in the city. That had been a different world. The romance and rhythm of that life had collapsed. Then, gradually, I became accustomed to life in the rural village. I wore village clothes, went to the market, planted the fields and fed the wage workers. My life had changed completely in such a short time. I was still very young now, but my days all seemed gloomy and meaningless.

Once in a while, we would go to visit my Great Uncle and his family in Mirzapur village. They were renting a small house from the Agriculture Office, near the canal. We wanted to go to their house every day, to spend some time talking and gossiping with our cousins. But that couldn't happen, given the distance, and our busy work schedules. Still, sometimes my older sister along with me and a younger brother would to go their house, walking there in the full heat of the sun. It gave all of us a sweet feeling when we got together with our cousin-sisters. We were all around the same age. We understood each other's feelings of happiness and sorrow, joy and pain. We would enjoy reminiscing together about our golden days - although the uncertainty and anxiety of our current situation never really left us.

My elder cousin-brother, who had planted brinjals with me, would also come there with us sometimes. He had been teaching at Bagerhat college before the Pakistani Army, as part of occupying the whole of East Pakistan, made moves to take over Bagerhat city, leading to panic among the city's residents, who began to flee the city en masse. At that time, my cousin-brother also fled the city, going first to his childhood home in Jhenaidah District. But, seeing that his family had all fled from there, he moved on to our common ancestral village. Before March, he had been offered a job in the Pakistani military, but he had declined it, seeing the deterioration of conditions in East Bengal under Pakistani rule.

After taking control of the whole country in May, the Pakistani army was able to gather a number of Bengali associates. Groups of them often patrolled the area around our village. In late May, the patrols began focussing their attention on our house. This was to be expected, because my uncle had been elected a member of the National Assembly in the 1970 elections. We lived in fear of what they might decide to do. One afternoon, the sound of a jeep was heard in the village, from a distance. At that moment the villagers started crying out, and running this way and that across the village. "The army!" they cried. They were confused and frightened. It was a terrible situation – they were completely unprepared for this. Who would flee to where, nobody knew. Everyone went crazy. My father gathered our whole family and we ran off urgently, to be gone before the Army arrived. My youngest brother and my sisters were very afraid of the Army. We walked four miles, to reach the house of a maternal relative. I was very sad to see my siblings having to make this tiring and frightened journey.

They also understood full well that these sufferings were not going to end soon. When we reached Bagbari village, we learned that the Army had been causing disturbances here too. It was said that the Army might soon attack the nearby Ponti Market. It looked as if we would never find peace. Although the Pakistani Army and its personnel came from far away, from a different country, it seemed that they had now added even the small villages in our country to their list of places to monitor and try to control. Wherever we might go, then, fear would not stop following us. All our efforts seemed to be in vain.

We stayed in Bagbari village for three or four days, restlessly. There was no one there whom we knew. Our prospects did not seem to be improving. We were still living in a place of fear. I spent my time roaming here and there, full of sadness.

Then, one day, Brother Rashid unexpectedly came from our village to talk to us. Brother Rashid had been orphaned at the age of 12 or 13, and come to live with us. Since then, Rashid had always called my father and mother "Father" and "Mother." However, because of the strong emphasis on biological parentage in Islam, he could only become an unofficial member of our family. He used to do a lot of small chores around the house for us. When we left Dhaka, he came to the village with us. His birth family had come from Faridpur, but he had no living relatives there. Now he came to my father, and said, "Father, let's go back to the village. There is no fear there. The army has not arrived there, nor will they come soon."

My father agreed to the idea, and the next day we returned to our village. Other former residents were returning there too. When we got back home, we breathed a sigh of relief, thinking, "Our troubles are manageable now, at least for the time being."

But, a month later, and again a few weeks after that, there were to be more moments of panic, resulting in temporary migrations to other villages. We would stay here and stay there, facing troubles and danger, and never really feeling safe anywhere. Looking back on those times now, however, I cannot but be grateful for the solidarity and generosity of the people in all those villages, who always offered to share with us whatever food they could spare, and gave us places to sleep in their houses.

On the evening after our return from Bagbari Village, we were glad to hear Nazu Uncle's father, Alimuddin, whom we called Grandfather, sounding the azan[10] for the Maghrib[11] prayer, from the

---

[10] An "azan" is a call to prayer
[11] Sunset

village mosque, in his sweet voice. (The father of my friends Reza and Yusuf, who was a mullah, also made these calls in a lovely voice, when it was his turn). As we listened to it, our minds became calm and cool. Now it felt as if one day everything would be OK. There is a bird called the pied crested cuckoo, that is known for eagerly, but patiently, waiting for rain during dry periods, and rushing to taste the first raindrops when rain finally comes. That night, I looked forward to hearing the news on the radio, with an eagerness matching that of a thirsty pied crested cuckoo.

The villagers would gather at the Mongla Brother's Medical Dispensary, near the mosque, after the prayers. There, we used to hear the BBC News, with special bulletins from Mark Tully, and Kolkata Radio's bulletins from Devdulal Bandyopadhyay. These announcers became a symbol of hope for us. After hearing their bulletins, we would return cheerfully to our house in the night. The next day, however, remembering the stark realities of our situation, we would feel the optimism inspired by those programs beginning to fade away, and would become glum once again.

Those in the village who had had office jobs before the March 25 atrocities, tended to feel especially confused and restless. Would they ever be able to return to their jobs? What would happen to them? - They really had no idea.

None of those former office job holders had gone to seek other, similar jobs. Where would they go? The state of the country did not seem to be favorable to them. It was true that reports from

Dhaka Radio indicated that things were now peaceful and normal around the country. Offices, schools, and colleges had all been reopened, they said. They called for people to come and take the jobs. Nobody believed them.

From over the border, Kolkata Radio reported that a Bangladeshi provisional government in exile had been established, and was requesting that other countries recognize it. That radio station also reported that there would soon be a new Bangladeshi government radio station which would transmit news and bulletins. Hearing these contradictory reports, the former office job holders were very confused. They could not decide what to do. The reports from Kolkata Radio were inspiring, but no signs of the reported changes could be seen locally. They wondered why no other countries had recognized the Bangladesh provisional government in exile, and why it seemed that the government in exile had failed to arrange for training for freedom fighters. If no such fighters were being trained, then it seemed that Pakistan was likely to prevail.

Two of these former office job holders, my father and his cousin, our Ranga Uncle (who was Black Uncle's brother), came to the decision that they would return to Dhaka. Despite all the uncertainty about what was happening in the country, they decided they wanted to go back there. Their decision really hurt me. I was wondering, if they left, how the life of our family in the village could be maintained. I felt very disappointed and sad. But they had made their decision, and would go. At the end of May, the two of them, risking their lives, set out to return to Dhaka. On the eve of their departure, my father said to me, "Be well. If I get a chance, I will come back. Try not to be upset. I'm sorry you will all be without a guardian."

After they left, the house felt very empty. It was as if the roof over all of our heads had disappeared. We were now a house full of kids, with no guardian. We were now just a house full of kids, with two women. As the oldest boy – though just in my 17th year – I was now considered to be responsible for looking after our family.

More than two months had passed since we left Dhaka, and the country's situation had not improved. Pakistani forces had begun to spread out to the villages and smaller towns in April. In the rural areas, many villages had been burned down. Many youths had been abducted. The people were oppressed. Hindus had begun to leave the country in large numbers. Most of the Hindus from the villages near us had left their homes, and become refugees in India. The waves of out-migration from the country were like flash floods. Popular frustration was growing day by day. No new reports were coming in from the BBC, or Kolkata Radio.

But there was a glimmer of hope in this dark atmosphere. We had heard from Kolkata Radio that an independent Bengali radio station would soon be established, and would broadcast its programs, on a regular basis, from its own broadcasting center. The joy this news had brought to us was akin to what we would feel on seeing the special new crescent moon, that signals both the end of Ramadan's sometimes agonizingly long month of hunger and thirst, and the beginning of the festivities of Eid. All around East Pakistan, there had been much resistance to Pakistani domination, ever since the atrocities of the 25th of March. But the people's fight had been unplanned and unorganized. Now that a provisional government in exile had been formed, the resistance would, we thought, surely be better organized.

The family of my Great Uncle returned to our village, bringing with them the family of the Principal of the Cadet College, in the first week of June. It was good to be close to our cousin-sisters. It gave us courage, to be able to spend time with more family, at home. At the time when we fled to Bagbari village, fearing the arrival of the army, Great Uncle's family had taken shelter in Mirzapur village. Soon after that, Great Uncle himself had departed from that village to go to India and join the freedom struggle. He was an extremely self-confident, strong, and courageous man. He had been a captain in the Pakistan Army in the fifties. We knew that he would not be able to accept a life of fleeing here and there in the country. He was bound to go join the war, the struggle for independence. This meant that he had to leave his family. He would walk about fifty miles across the country to get to India. Although he could easily have chosen to rejoin the Cadet College, he was compelled to go, and help liberate the country.

The monsoon rains came early. In April, the expected storms had not come, which meant that the soil was thirsty, but also meant that storms had not blown the roofs off of houses, or uprooted trees. With the heavy monsoon rains arriving in June, the villagers found relief from the intense heat of summer, and rural life now began to return to normal, with the endless monsoon rains. Many people thought of the heavy rains as a blessing. They thought that the muddiness and slipperiness of the roads would disrupt the movements of

Pakistani troops. Life generally went on as normal for us in this situation. To avoid spoiling our clothes, we would go to the market daily wearing our Lungis[12] slightly high. Then, after marketing, we would return to the village in the evening. We did not like walking to the market along the muddy, slippery road every day. But we had to go. Because Mother wouldn't be able to cook for us if we didn't bring home the provisions.

Some weeks passed in this way. Then, one day, through some contacts, we heard that Great Uncle had been appointed director of the youth camp, in the western sector of the government in exile. Many people were in contact with him. His wife and daughters were secretly preparing to go and stay with him in India. But their trip was delayed because of the situation of the principal's family. The principal's wife had received word that her husband had been killed by the Pakistan Army when they captured Jhenaidah. He had previously sent his wife and children to the village, with the family of Great Uncle, knowing that his family was in danger in Jhenaidah, but believing that, because he had grown up speaking Urdu, in India, and was fluent in it, he personally would be safe there. The principal's wife and her daughter depended heavily on my Auntie (Great Uncle's wife) to help them cope, after learning of his death. Auntie, feeling that this helpless family could not be left floating in this situation, declared that she would not go to India until this family was well settled. The

---

[12] A lungi is a type of sarong.

extended family decided that Black Uncle would take the principal's family to Dhaka. Then he would return to the village, and then accompany Great Uncle's family to India.

The principal's little boy had captured our hearts. We loved him very much. He was about five or six years old. He had mingled very well with the villagers' own little boys. They used to play together all day long under the open sky. He was at home in the village's natural environment. He had not yet been told about his father's death. As we looked at him, our hearts were filled with pain. Just how cruel a war could be, came home to us when we looked at this little boy. He cried too, on the day when his family left the village. He did not want to leave it. It had become dear to him over his two-month stay. We were all very sad when the family left. I walked a long way behind their horse cart. So did his little friends. But we could not accompany them all the way to their destination. A family that been part of our extended family for many days would now be far away from us. Sometimes people have to fight for others' happiness as well as their own, because the sorrows and pains of different families are essentially the same.

Black Uncle returned to the village, having taken the principal's family to Dhaka safely. Now, it was the turn of Great Uncle's family to depart. A horse cart had been hired for a week later. The family's goods were packed up over the course of a few days. Their preparations were now complete. Great Auntie would soon be leaving us, along with her daughters. She asked to take my older sister with her. Young Bengali women were in great danger of being tortured and raped by Pakistani soldiers in the current situation in our country, so she would be safer in India. Nevertheless, my mother said, "No."

We had shared a lot of happiness, joy and sorrow with Great Auntie and her daughters. On the eve of their departure, we became very sad. We didn't know if we would ever see them again. The future is a place we can't see. We worried about how they would get across the border, having to travel through our calamity -ridden country. As they left, Black Uncle told us, "Don't worry. I'll come back soon, after leaving them in India." But Black Uncle would not return to the village that year.

Great Uncle's family were in tears as they left. Their departure left us badly dispirited, for a while. We had lived with them, played cards with them, eaten meals together, and spent time gossiping. Now they were gone. There was a new emptiness in our lives. In our village, our once joyful home, we now felt isolated.

Many of our family, along with hundreds of thousands of other Bengalis, were now finding shelter in India. Besides Great Uncle's family, the family of my uncle who'd been elected a member of the National Assembly (MNA) had also gone to

India, we now heard - after facing a lot of trouble in Magura District.

The son of another uncle had been in the village with us for quite some time. He then went to join the College of Bagerhat as a lecturer, but saw that everybody from there had fled to India. My cousin-brother Ranzu, who had been an entertaining and enjoyable companion in the village despite the hardships he had experienced, and who had previously stayed in our house in Dhaka for a few days when he was finishing his degree, also now left the village to join Bagerhat's Prafulla Chandra College, as a Professor. We missed him very much too. Now the whole house seemed empty. My father and Ranga Uncle were in Dhaka. Three uncles had joined the government in exile in India. Black Uncle's and Great Uncle's families were in India. It seemed that most of our large, close-knit family had now been torn away from us. This was very hard to take. I took some comfort in wandering about and gossiping with the men I had come to think of as my village grandfather, uncle, and brothers, and who were still around. But even with their company, my depression did not go away. I was filled with frustration and pain.

CHAPTER 6: JULY

I was now the oldest male from our immediate family at our now too-empty house. We did have one uncle in the house, whose name was Monowar (he was a cousin of my father's, and a brother to Ranga Uncle and Black Uncle). He had lived in that house for a long time. But he was the only one. Many days had passed since my father had left us for Dhaka. He had not returned, and we'd had no news of him. We were experiencing a financial crisis. Father was not sending money to us. Our stock of rice – from the previous year's crop - had run out. Rice cultivation in the village had resumed with the onset of the rainy season. But we were now in a food crisis. My mother did her best to cook for us, using the fragments of rice that the villagers had saved from the previous year's harvest. Every day now, Mother gave us tiny servings of such broken rice – which the villagers called "rice waste" - with our meals. We had never eaten broken rice before. My little sisters and brothers often refused to eat it. They would sometimes say to Mother, "Why is the rice so soft? Rice like this cannot be eaten." Mother did not reply to them. She silently wiped her eyes with her apron. We, the older children, were left speechless in these moments. We had seen that it made Mother sad, just to see us eating this stuff. Maybe Mother wept because she was remembering the life we had had in Dhaka a few months ago. Her brother's friends used to come by our house there. My sisters' friends would also come by. We often hosted small celebrations there. My siblings and I used to play with our friends from the neighborhood. We would go with our friends to hear concerts. On the twenty-first of February, we would go to Shaheed Minar together, to pay tribute to the martyrs of the Bengali language movement. My father's friends would come to our house and sing songs. That way of life had been very different. We had never imagined that the state of the country would change so much over the course of a few days. Now, when my sisters and brothers and I would lie down on our beds after eating dinner, we would often reminisce about our past times, in Dhaka. Eventually, as the monsoon rains dropping on the tin roof of our village house played their sad melody, we would slowly fall asleep in the dark night.

The food crisis was just one of our problems. The sufferings of the country as a whole were not over. More bad news came to us. Razakar[13] forces had been formed in the country. The Razakars were Bengali people who had been recruited to help with the Pakistan Army's domination of the country. These traitorous people voluntarily registered their names with the Razakar forces. One man from our

---

[13] The Razakars were a paramilitary force raised by the Pakistan Army during the Bangladesh Liberation War in 1971, to help suppress the Bengali freedom fighters. The force was composed of anti-liberation Bengalis and so-called Biharis (Urdu-speaking non-Bengali immigrants). The first Razakar unit was raised in Khulna in May, 1971. Derived from the Arabic word rīdkār (رضاکار,) meaning "volunteer."

village joined up with them. Since the Razakar forces had begun to be formed, in May, villages and market places had started being destroyed by fire. Abductions of, and violence against, young people suspected of opposing the regime, had increased. Parents and guardians of young girls worried about what would happen to them, even in their own houses. These Razakars were Bengali people oppressing other Bengalis, and further exacerbating the cruelty of the Pakistani regime, and its evil effects on our lives. The Razakars showed the Pakistani soldiers ways to effectively invade the villages. Once they entered a village, they would harass and threaten ordinary people there. Bengalis in general were fed up with both the Razakars and the Army. But we had no alternative but to endure the situation in silence. We constantly suffered from panic and fear.

Then there was another weird night, and another lengthy family trek, this time in the dark. The evening Azan and prayer had been completed. I, along with mother, sisters, and brothers, had just sat down to eat dinner. Suddenly, we heard someone running up to our house. Then a man rushed into the house and told us, "You should flee now. Pakistani troops are on their way here, and will attack your house." Even though we'd just started eating, we ran out of the house and down to the village's gathering place, by the mosque. We were very scared. We were glad to meet up with Nazu Uncle (a cousin-brother of Black Uncle) on our way. He had been rushing toward our house to lead us away. When he saw us, he just said, "Hurry, let's go. Come with me."

Once again, having left our house in a panic, we, including my little brothers and sisters, began to walk along a long muddy path. The elderly mother- and father-in-law of Ranga Uncle were with us. How they were managing in this situation, I didn't know. We had not had our dinner. We were all suffering extreme hardship. We walked two miles through the night, and eventually reached Nazu Uncle's house, in his ancestral village. We went to bed late in the night, exhausted in mind and body, hungry, and aching from our anxious flight from our home village. But the Gorai River, which flowed by the side of the village, comforted us at night with the music of its flowing, which was like a flute being played compassionately for us, in the sad tones of our family's life.

We had begun to be accustomed to living in several different villages. And the people in these villages didn't hesitate to give us shelter and food. But we really felt that we were not safe anywhere anymore.

Two days after we left our home village, we heard that the Army had not actually shown up there. So, the next day, we returned there. When we'd been back home for two days, a stranger unexpectedly came to our house. He had a bag hanging from the handlebar of his bicycle. He rang our doorbell. I went to open the door, and then I realized that he was a postman. He gave me a letter. Given the state of our country, I was surprised to see that the post was actually being delivered. I tried to think of who might be sending me a letter. My name was on it, so I opened it. I was surprised to see that it was from a friend from our old Green Road neighborhood in Dhaka. She probably, I realized, had gotten my address from my father, who was staying in Dhaka now. She wrote:

"How are you? Do you remember me, or have you forgotten everything? I haven't forgotten you. Your father came to our house. We heard everything about your whole family. It must be very difficult, really, having to stay out there in the village, away from Dhaka. I felt very bad, hearing about all your distress, from your father. Though Dhaka looks a bit normal these days, it is not the same city now, as it was six months ago. I sometimes remember how it used to be. You and your bunch of friends no longer walk by our house. Nobody plays cricket, any longer, in the field across the road from us. I also sit idle and alone all day these days, in a melancholy mood. I find I that I can't even read. Are you going to sit for the Grade 12 examinations? I asked Uncle (your father). He said your studies had been stopped, and wouldn't start again until the freedom struggle was over. So, if this freedom struggle continues for a long time, does that mean you won't study anymore? Stay well. Awaiting your reply."

Reading the letter left me feeling numb. She and I were the same age, and had passed Grade 10 together. During our examinations, her mother used to invite me to eat at their place before going to the examination hall. My mother had gone to her family's village, then, to mourn the death of her mother (my grandmother), and so was not cooking breakfast for me. After eating, my friend and I would go to the examination hall together. My father used to give us a lift to the hall in his car. After reading her letter, I fell into distressed rumination. I was thinking, what am I going to do? If the war continues for years, then what will I do? Should I give up on studying? I had grim thoughts about my future, and felt very frustrated.

CHAPTER 7: AUGUST

The Razakars' activities were being stepped up. We heard that a Razakar man would come to our village. We felt less and less safe in my paternal grandparents' village. So, my mother decided that we should all go to her own parents' house, which was in a village in Kushtia District, 10 miles away. Which meant that our family had to make another long trek on foot, to that village. (The elder of my younger brothers, however, rebelled against the plan, and didn't come with us. Brother Rashid also remained in the paternal village.)

There, my two maternal uncles were very busy with working in support of the liberation war. They used to walk all around their village at night, asking everyone about any freedom fighters who might have come by. The older uncle was the chairman of the local union council. He was a very bold man. He was popularly known as Batul Chairman. Nobody called him by his real name – Aminul Islam. He was very active in the local union. The younger uncle, whom we called *Kanthal* ("jackfruit") Uncle, wasn't any less active than his brother. Kanthal Uncle had left Dhaka in late March, to move to the village. He also kept busy. This uncle had lived with us in Dhaka for nine years. He had been very politically active. My mother had been very frightened by the Pakistan Army's crackdown on 25th March. She worried that Pakistani troops would target my uncle, and kill him, since he'd been so involved in politics; so she encouraged him to go out to the village. He had a Chinese Phoenix bike. He made the trip from Dhaka to Kushtia District, with that bicycle. On his way, he saw that thousands of other people were also fleeing in the direction of Kushtia, by way of Dhaka's Gabtoli bridge, after 27th March. The road was so crowded with people, that cycling was impossible. So he was forced to walk his bike along the road. After he got through Savar Thana, it took him two days to cycle to the port of Aricha Ghat.

When he arrived at the ferry terminal there, he saw that its operations had been shut down. But the ferry operators soon restarted their services, having seen that a lot of customers were ready to pay for them. Kanthal Uncle, after crossing the Jamuna river on a ferry, and then passing through Pangsha Thana, arrived in his home village of Kumarkhali. On his way, he had seen thousands of people heading to Kushtia Town, where the East Pakistan Rifles (EPR) were engaged in a battle with the Pakistan Army. The EPR forces had cordoned off the Pakistan Army from the area of Kushtia District School since 2nd April. Villagers were coming from far away, in great numbers, carrying rice, molasses, and bread, to feed the EPR fighters. The battle there was very dramatic. The EPR troops were fighting against the very well-organized and well-equipped Pakistan Army, at great risk to their lives. Rural Bengalis, deeply impressed by their courage, decided to support them, by feeding them. This was an unforgettable event for rural Bengalis. What emotion! What excitement! Kushtia must be liberated!

We had heard about this battle from Kolkata Radio in April, when we were in Dhaka. But we didn't know whether to believe the news story. Then, later, hearing this story from our uncle, we realized that it was completely true, even if the reports from East Pakistan Radio were almost always full of lies.

Unfortunately, the EPR could not retain possession of Kushtia. The EPR's resistance was crushed by the Pakistan Army. Surviving fighters fled elsewhere to find safety. Many of the fighters had died.

The Battle of Kushtia had a broad impact on my maternal grandparents' region. The number of participants in the liberation struggle began to increase, and trained freedom fighters began to be effectively organized in that rural area. Meanwhile, the Razakars also increased their activities in support of the Pakistan Army. Another new political group, of self-styled "Leftists," had also been formed, and begun to make propaganda against the liberation war. It was difficult for my family to stay at my maternal uncles' home, because some of my mother's cousin-brothers had connections with the "leftists". Their ways of thinking were very different from ours. Sometimes leaders of the "leftists" would come to the uncles' house from elsewhere and hold meetings in the small one-room meeting house next to the maternal uncles' house. One day I heard one of them say, "The struggle will have to be a very long one. You know that Vietnam has continued to struggle for a long time. We, too, will have to fight for a long time. If we don't do that, true liberation will never come. Because, the current war is not a people's war. It is a fight between two right-wing groups." These "leftists" were pro-Chinese. China was fully supporting Pakistani domination in Bengal. Hearing statements like this from their leaders upset me. I thought, "So many people are dying here, but they don't care about that. They want more war." I understood why they were seeking to prolong the war: they supported Pakistani domination. While the Razakars were directly and openly opposing the freedom struggle, the "leftists" were opposing it in an underhanded way. So I felt that I could not stay at the maternal uncles' house any longer. A few days after we arrived there, I said goodbye to my mother, and returned to my paternal grandparents' house alone, walking ten miles from the maternal village.

Back in my paternal grandparents' now nearly-empty house, I felt lonely. Until recently, there had been quite a number of people staying in the house. Now, besides me, only my younger brother was in the house. I had no father, no mother, no cousins, and only one sibling there. Ranga Uncle's family, it is true, were also nearby, in another house on our courtyard. But, in an attempt to relieve my loneliness, I would roam around from house to house during the day. A few fellow-villagers, whom I called "Grandfather," "Brother," and "Uncle," became my constant companions. We would go to the village market together, sometimes chatting along the way, and generally roam around together. Sometimes we would play cards into the night, while listening to the radio news. Though these companions were generally four or five years older than me, we had close relationships. But my sense of emptiness still did not go away. I wondered, how long would I go on feeling this way?

In this depressed state of mind, one day I had a quarrel with my younger brother. It almost turned into a physical fight, but that did not quite happen. We just kept on quarrelling and shouting for a while. I asked him to study the schoolbooks we had brought from Dhaka for him, but he did not do so. And he said, "I don't see you reading any books!" I was the elder brother, so I didn't respond to his comment. It was mainly my continually telling him to study that led to the quarrel. We spent one day like this, and then mostly stopped talking to each other, and took to sleeping separately, in different rooms. A few days after the quarrel, I left the house, as usual, to go and chat with my village companions. At midday, I came back to the house, but found that my brother was gone. I waited for him, thinking he would come home to eat lunch. But he did not turn up. When evening fell, he still wasn't there. I went out to search for him in the village, but couldn't find him. Then I came back to the house, but I worried about him all night. The next day, I went to the market with my village "Grandfather," to buy foodstuffs. As we were walking there, a man silently approached me, and then told me that a young man from the village had seen my younger brother crossing the railway tracks at Halsa Station, near the Indian border; and then seen him crossing the border into India.

I had worried that my brother might do that one day - flee to India, to be trained as a freedom fighter. And now he had done it. He was very courageous. He was just fifteen years old then, two years younger than me. It seemed like he felt no attachment to, or responsibility for, his family. He had gone off to war just like that, without saying anything to me. I worried about how I would tell my mother about this. What could I say to her? I was very depressed now. He was just a young boy, I thought. What did he understand about war? Sometimes I thought that he'd probably just had a craving for adventure, and that had led him to go and get involved in the war. Other times, I believed that he'd genuinely wanted to contribute to the struggle for our country's independence. Sometimes I would reproach myself for not displaying the kind of courage he had displayed, and feel proud of him, for this brave move. But, it was mainly my responsibilities to my family that were keeping me from participating in the liberation struggle. How could he have just gone off like that, to fight, when his little brothers and sisters were still at home? Whatever his motivation might have been, I really was alone now, with no mother, brothers, sisters, or father around.

My loneliness was intense. My attachments to my family were strong and deep, despite my young age. I now thought about my younger brother all the time. We had grown up together. He was born soon after me. So, we'd spent a lot of time together. We had studied in the same school. We used to wear the same clothes, and spend the whole day together. We used to sleep in the same bed at night. Often, we would quarrel even there, before going to sleep. Still, if he went somewhere, and someone gave him a sweet guava fruit, he would save it, and bring it home for me. When he was in a good mood, he was ready to give me everything, but when he was angry he would swear at me, using very dirty language.

As I lay alone on my bed on the eastern side of the house, my thoughts wandered in distress and confusion. I gazed out the wooden window, at a fir tree standing alone, some distance away. My current solitary, lonely life was like that of this tree, I thought. Family separation was a cruel effect of war. Being unable to communicate with other members of my family made life seem bleak. This war was a terrible disaster for us.

The month of August was almost over now. Other than my younger brother, Brother Rashid had also been there with me for a long period. But, ten or twelve days ago, Brother Rashid had gone to his own parents' house. I had expected him to return within ten days, but he had not come back yet. He really was like family to us. He had come with us from Dhaka to the village during this very difficult time of our lives. In the absence of my father, mother, siblings, and younger brother, Brother Rashid had been, for a while, my best companion. He would go to the market, cook, and do anything else that was needed. Now I felt helplessly morose. The heavy Monsoon rains, which usually only last for about one month, had started in May, and were still falling now, in August. Late one night, when I was in bed, and being lulled to sleep by the sound of the rains falling on the tin roof, I suddenly heard a faint voice that seemed to be calling to me from some distance away. When I heard it a second time, I sat up, fully alert. This time, I could hear that it was Brother Rashid, who was approaching the house, and calling my name! What joy! I felt like rushing out to welcome him. It seemed he'd been my closest friend during this difficult time. I realized that I loved him strongly and deeply. And now I felt that there was no real separation between me and anything else in this world. The misery of my solitary life and loneliness diminished greatly, with the return of Brother Rashid.

Just as the return of Brother Rashid was filling me with joy, I also received a letter from my father – his first communication since he left the village. In the letter, he mostly expressed concern about us. He cautioned us to be careful, and wrote a little about various family matters. He concluded the letter with a few personal messages for me: "I have sent you a Philips radio, along with some money. Give the money to your mother. I wonder how you have been, and how you are passing your days... I left nothing for you when I left for Dhaka. It is really a big worry for me. Try to manage as long as you can with the money I sent. I'll come and see you soon." These concluding words brought me to tears.

Three or four days after that, Ranga Uncle himself also returned to the village from Dhaka – yet another immensely joyful event for me - I now expected that, soon, we would all be feeling the sense of security that comes from having a good father figure around. And I was also very happy to have the Philips radio that my father had sent me, and to be able to listen to the news.

A vigorous training program for freedom fighters had begun in India. Young men wanting to be trained had begun crossing the border into India, in great numbers, in July. Many of them were from villages near ours. Three or four boys from our own village went there. One of my friends from the village, with whom I used to wander about, gossiping, had also crossed the border to be trained there. It seemed that there was a great wave of such young men, spontaneously volunteering to join the struggle.

One day, at about noon, I saw two young men, sixteen or seventeen years old, strolling through the courtyard of our house. They were strangers to me, and I wanted to know who they were, so I went out and asked them," Who are you? Where do you come from?"

One of them replied, "We are from Agunpara village. We walked here from there this morning."

I asked, "Why?"

The young man looked around him, and then said, in a soft voice, "We're going to go to India for training. Please write a letter to your uncle for me; I'll take it to him."

I asked, "Who told you that my uncle can get you into a freedom fighter training program?"

He said, "Everyone knows that your uncle is in charge of the Youth Training Camp there!"

I said, "But I can't write a letter to him for you! What if you are caught on your way there?"

He replied, "Don't worry. Nobody will know. We'll just take your letter home with us, and then tonight, we'll secretly start for India from there."

I said, "No! That's no good! The Pakistan Army will find out."

They said, "Once we make it to India, there may be many more guys who will come to talk to you, to take letters to your uncle there."

I realized that these young men were ready to go to the training camp, and could not be stopped now.

In this way, I also found myself involved in the liberation war. After those two young men left, I would write letters to my Great Uncle for some other young men too. I wrote the letters that these young men requested, but did so fearfully – remembering that Great Uncle could get terribly angry sometimes.

As the first two young men were leaving, another, slightly older, young man appeared from the direction of the pond. As he approached the house, I realized that I recognized him. He was a friend of my cousin. I shouted out to him, 'Hey, Jafar brother, what brings you here? How did you know where our house was?"

He replied, "It wasn't easy to find you, but finally, I have! Where is your mother?"

I said, "About ten miles away, in my maternal grandfather's village."

He said, "Let's go there."

I said, "It's noon now, and it's so hot! How can we go now? We'd have to walk for two to three hours."

He said, "No problem! Let's just go."

The free and open conversations that local villagers used to have among themselves could no longer be heard, and the villages seemed almost silent. Everyone felt uneasy. As the aspiring freedom fighters took shelter in these villages, the residents of the villages would put on fixed, inscrutable faces, and stay very quiet, for fear that the Razakars would come to know about the young freedom fighters. If information about the young men leaked out, they would be in, great danger. So, people would creep about like lizards. But the Razakars hadn't actually attacked anyone in the village for some days, and I had begun to contemplate bringing my mother, brothers, and sisters, back to the paternal village. When Jafar brother came and urged me to walk to the maternal village with him, it seemed to offer me an opportunity to put my plans into action. We departed in the early afternoon.

We talked a lot during our ten-mile walk.

I asked him, "Where have you been for the past couple of months? In Ishwardi?" (where he had been posted the last time I spoke to him.)

He said, "No. In Kolkata."

I said, "In Kolkata!? You mean you just came from India?"

He said, "Yes. And I'll be going back soon. There are things happening here now that I wanted to find out about, and I thought I should stop by your village and see you. How are you passing your days?"

I ignored his question, and kept asking him about his own plans, "Why are you going back there?"

He said, "We are making transceivers and walkie talkies. Together with one other electrical engineer, I am designing transceivers and walkie talkies. The freedom fighters will use them in the war."

Hasibur Rahman, a young professor at the University of Engineering and Technology in Dhaka, had had experience in making transmitters in 1969. He was now using that experience. And he had found a partner in Jafar brother. Prior to the start of the war, in 1970-71, Jafar brother had been working in the power house of Ishwardi sub-district, in Pabna District, as an assistant engineer of the sub-district's Electricity Development Board. After the army's atrocities in March, he had decided to join the thousands of other Bengalis who were fleeing to India. In India, he reported to the embassy of the Provisional Government of Bangladesh.

In India, Jafar and Professor Rahman met with members of the Provisional Government of Bangladesh. Those government members had been communicating with several Indian engineers, who had offered their support and cooperation to the exile government. Together, they found a space in Kolkata in which to establish the exile government's radio station. There, they went to work on producing transmitters. Unfortunately, the quartz crystals necessary for this work were not

available in Kolkata. Professor Rahman was
disappointed to learn this, but he did not give up. In
the end, the provisional government's ambassador
to England, Mr. Hossain Ali, contacted John
Stonehouse, who had, the previous year, been the
Minister of Posts and Telecommunications in the
United Kingdom's Labour government; and
Stonehouse eventually took two dozen of these
crystals from England to India, and handed them
over to the provisional government's embassy.

So, now I asked Jafar brother, "Have you
managed to produce some of the things you wanted
to make?"

He said – "There are thirty transceivers and
forty walkie talkies that have been made. The range
of the transceivers is thirty to sixty miles, and the
walkie talkies' range is eight to ten miles."

Jafar brother had returned to Bangladesh,
crossing the Indian border, to check how well the
provisional government's radio station's programs
were reaching listeners in Bangladesh, and what
the range of the transceivers was inside the
country. His journey was a very adventurous,
night-time one. If he'd been caught, he would have
been killed.

We reached my mother's parents' village in the
evening. Everyone in our family was happy to see
us. We all listened to what Jafar had to tell us about
developments in the liberation movement. In the
old days, when we were in Dhaka, he had often
come to our house there with a cousin-brother of

mine. He had developed a close relationship with our family then. This time, he spent the night in the village house, and then returned to Kolkata the following day. We all appreciated the fact that this twenty-six-year-old, who had had a good job, had left it to help free his motherland.

When he was leaving, I asked him, "Will you come back soon?"

He said, "Yes, I'll see you soon. The transceivers and walkie talkies will be used very soon in the war in the border region. Because the war will start soon."

When he was gone, we all missed him.

CHAPTER 8: SEPTEMBER

It had been more than a month since I'd had any news of my mother, sisters, and little brothers in the maternal grandparents' village. Soon after Jafar and I arrived there, we learned that, during that month, both of my maternal uncles and several of my cousins had continued to keep very busy with their activities in support of the freedom struggle. My older uncle had gone to India about a week before we arrived, but had returned after a few days. The uncles' younger cousins had not yet returned from their training in India. Soon after we arrived, my older uncle told me, "You should take your mother and siblings, and go back to your other village. The Army made camp in the village of Durbachara near our house, and the Razakars have been gathering with them there. They are going to every village, hunting down freedom fighters. Like you, we have also been fleeing from one village to another. Go, as soon as you can!"

The Pakistani Military had, it turned out, begun wreaking havoc in the adjacent villages. When my older uncle, the chairman of the union council for all of these villages, returned from his visit to India, the villagers hoped that he would do something to help improve their safety, or at least help them unite to take positive action. As soon as he arrived, he established contact with most of the freedom fighters in the union, and found out where they were all staying. Then, he started arranging for food and shelter for them. He also consulted with them about the kinds of actions that they planned to carry out. Teams of well-trained freedom fighters were returning from India. They were becoming more and more active all around the country, but especially in Kushtia District. All this activity drove the Pakistan Army crazy. They began hunting everywhere for the freedom fighters. When they failed to find them, they would burn down houses, and torture innocent people, in the villages. Ten days ago, freedom fighters had had a battle with Razakars and Biharis based in the region. The Razakars and Biharis had gathered in Bongshitola village, which was next to Durbachara village, to plan their looting of the villagers' property. After some freedom fighters heard about this, they became determined to disrupt the Razakars' operations. A group of them assembled near the river, and launched some counterattacks on the Razakars and Biharis. Four freedom fighters had died in this battle.

Because of all the heavy fighting, and the Army's burning down of most of the houses in so many villages, the residents of the neighboring villages had been badly scared, and many of them had fled the area. The villages had become deserted and empty. One day, some of the residents of our village saw the bodies of four deceased freedom fighters lying on the ground in Bongshitola village. There was no one there to bring them in and bury them. So the freedom fighters had not been buried. Bongshitola was next to my mother's parents' village, and also right next to the river. The day after the presence of the bodies was reported, Kanthal Uncle and two companions risked their lives, by getting into boats on the river, to get to the bodies. During the night, they managed, stealthily, to carry the four bodies to Durbachara village, near Bongshitola, and bury them secretly there. Kanthal Uncle returned home very late that night. The older uncle scolded him for taking on this risky operation. Most of the people in our house had no sleep that night. My mother, grandmother, and maternal great aunt, when they heard this dreadful story, started crying. I only heard the story later, after Jafar and I arrived in the village. The story certainly gave me pause. I murmured, "Who would endanger his life in this way?" But then I thought that taking care of the freedom fighters' bodies had been worth the risk. For them not to be buried was unthinkable!

Two days after Jafar brother and I arrived there, I, along with my family, left my maternal grandparents' village. Keeping in mind the food shortages that we had recently suffered from, in the paternal village, we carried two sacks of paddy rice with us. The paddy rice needed, however, to be husked, before it could be cooked and eaten, which meant that my mother would have to boil the paddy in a large pot for over an hour, just like the local women in the village. When the paddy was finished boiling, she would spread it out evenly in the yard, by walking on it, to let it dry in the sun. Then she would, with the help of another woman, husk the dried paddy, using a traditional wooden foot-powered rice-pounding device. We had never seen Mother performing such typically rural, physically demanding labor before. She had been a city woman since the age of seventeen, when she got married. Even as a young girl, growing up in her father's village, she hadn't done this kind of work. Her father had worked in the Government Railway Department, and then, after retiring, become the headmaster of a school. Her childhood and adolescence had passed in relative affluence, with no need for her to perform such tasks. We had seen her as a well-bred, sophisticated woman, not a village laborer. She would spend her time caring for her children, and supervising our activities. In our Dhaka house, most of the domestic chores were performed by hired help. Mother focused her attention on whether we went to school or not, whether we were studying, deciding what we would all eat, and arranging for shopping to be done at the market. Now, as we saw how she coped with these difficult circumstances, we began to also appreciate other aspects of her character, including her courage and adaptability, and her determination to make sure that all of our needs were met. Today, she appeared to us not just as a woman, but also as a warrior. Perhaps this shouldn't have surprised us, given that she had attended Bangobandhu Sheikh Mujibur Rahman's inspiring speech of 7th March, in the race course ground.

Every day we received warnings that the Razakars and the Pakistan Army were going to come and burn down our house. A few days passed without their showing up, but we still lived in a perpetual state of anxiety. One day, the man from our village who had joined the Razakars arrived in our village, with a group of soldiers, and some other Razakars, in the morning, at around 11:00

am. The village was in a mess, with people running around in panic. Mother was scared. She had previously sent me to the house of the village mollah to hide, and sent my sisters to another house. She always focused on protecting us, even at risk to her own life. On that day, Ranga Uncle was in the house. He had returned from Dhaka two or three days before.

The freedom fighters had brought magazines and newspapers with them, when they returned from their training in India. The newspaper was published by the exile government. Ranga Uncle had hidden all the newspapers by burying them in the ground near the cluster of bamboo trees. We had been expecting the Pakistan army to come to the village. Hearing the noise of our neighbors running around in panic, I realized that the army had indeed entered the village. From inside Mollah Uncle's house, I couldn't see the soldiers walking up to the front of our house, where Ranga Uncle was standing. Those who did see this were very fearful for him, that the soldiers would kill him. They talked to him for a long time, in Urdu, which he knew -- but the villagers near the house didn't, and couldn't understand his conversation with them. The soldiers stayed with him for more than half an hour, and then left the village. Once the soldiers were gone, the villagers and I all went and surrounded Ranga Uncle.

Everyone asked him a lot of questions. He told us, 'They came to burn down the house. They asked about my younger cousin-brother, the MNA (Member of Parliament).

'I told them, "He's not here. He has gone to India."'

The Pakistani soldiers had been ready to set fire to the house, using kerosene. They'd had a matchbox in their hands. Ranga Uncle had humbly asked them not to set fire to the house. And in the end, they let the house be, but asked Ranga Uncle to write to his brother, to tell him to come home.

And he told them, "Okay ".

The house had been saved because Ranga Uncle dealt calmly with the soldiers, speaking to them in their own language. When the soldiers and Razakars left the village, the villagers sighed with relief, and my sisters and I came out from the houses we were in, and hugged Ranga Uncle for a long time. But our heart palpitations had not stopped yet. Ranga Uncle had taken a great risk by staying there to talk to the soldiers. We didn't understand why. They might have killed him! Perhaps it was his love for his ancestral house that had motivated him.

The rains were still falling, but had lessened somewhat. The village roads were still very muddy, but it looked like the rain was now going to gradually decrease. Harvest time had arrived. The farmers had been preparing to harvest the rice.

Within seven to eight days, they would start. So, there would be no food crisis for us now. We were now able to shop at the market every day, with the money that Father had sent from Dhaka. The prices of food items at the market had also gone down a lot, almost as if we'd gone back to the time of the Moghul ruler Shaista Khan[14]. The reason for the price drops was that trading was now confined to a fixed, small area. Also, only limited amounts of money were in circulation. Thus, even with just a small amount of money, a family could live very well. We now had no problems in day-to-day transactions.

---

[14] Moghul governor of Bengal from 1664 to 1688.

Trained freedom fighters had started returning to the country during the months of August and September. They took shelter secretly in local villages, in small groups of two, three, or four. Raihan Uncle, from our own village, was one of those who had returned. It was now dawning on all of us that these newly trained freedom fighters were now really ready for war. This made me feel more optimistic for our country's future. One night, in mid-October, after everyone in the house had gone to bed, we suddenly heard the sound of footsteps near the house. It sounded like a large group of people was approaching. We were all afraid, and just kept lying quietly on our beds. Then we heard the voice of one of the village men that my siblings and I called "Grandfather." He was calling my name and saying, "Get up. Don't be afraid. It's your Grandpa Tabarek. Open the door."

We relaxed, and I went to open the door. I saw that there were ten to twelve young men standing there with Grandpa Tabarek. Their beards were unkempt, and their shirts shabby, and they were wearing lungis. They had rifles on their shoulders. Their SLRs (Self-loading rifles) were wrapped in shawls. Another of our neighbors, Motahar brother, also came in with them. Grandpa Tabarek said, "They've just returned from India, after receiving their training there. They're on their way to Pangsha, in Faridpur. Please give them some food to eat."

So now, for the first time, I was meeting some real, live, trained freedom fighters in person. Some of those thousands of crazy boys who'd volunteered themselves for the dangerous work of national liberation. Another of our neighbors, Motahar brother, also came in with the freedom fighters.

My mother cooked us all a dinner of rice, lentils and vegetables, and I wondered, will they enjoy eating a simple meal like that? We all sat down on the floor, as we normally did to eat dinner in the villages, and they ate happily, pushing up the sleeves of their shabby shirts, pushing their beards into their faces, and chatting while they ate, calling my mother 'Auntie' and my older sister 'Sister.' They cuddled my little brother. Their confident presence gave us courage. They were just teenagers. Sensing their strong commitment to their cause, and deep love for our country, I began to feel that the creation of an independent Bangladesh was inevitable. After they finished eating, they shook hands with us and began to make their way out, heading for Pangsha. Before leaving, they said to my mother and older sister, "Auntie, Sister, pray to Allah for us. If we survive, then we will see you again." All of us became very emotional — close to tears -- as they began to leave. They were still very young, I reflected, but they were setting a great example, by volunteering to sacrifice their lives to liberate the country. They were not expecting anything for themselves, but had vowed to do all they could to make sure their country became independent.

As the freedom fighters headed out into the night, together with Grandpa Tabarek and Motahar brother, they quietly handed me two hand grenades and two small landmines, whispering, "We are leaving these with you. They will be needed. We will be in touch with you over time, as we will be needing to bring arms and ammunition over from India regularly." Grandpa Tabarek and I hid the weapons in our house. It seemed that, in this way, I was becoming even more deeply involved in the country's liberation war. Grandpa Tabarek and Motahar brother then accompanied the freedom fighters as far as the Gorai river, near Katlagari Bazar, two miles away. The two of them returned to the village some hours later -- at about dawn.

After their departure, I cautiously turned to look at my mother's face. I could see that she was very worried. She angrily said to me, "If the Army finds out that freedom fighters have come to this house, then they will take you away and kill you. What is the need to be so brave?"

She really was afraid for me.

I told her, 'Don't be afraid. Nothing will happen.
'

My mother and siblings eventually came to know about the presence of the weapons. But our family wasn't actually going to do anything with them. Grandpa and I had just put them in the corner of the tin-roofed house. In the end, the freedom fighters never contacted us, or came to the house, again.

CHAPTER 10: **NOVEMBER**

Young freedom fighters from the neighboring
villages started coming to me. Some of the boys
who had taken letters from me to my Great Uncle,
to get training, came back to see me again. All of
these returnees carried copies of the Bengali
newspaper of the exile government with them.
There was reporting on the liberation war in these
newspapers.

Grandpa Tabarek, Motahar brother, Hashem
brother, Nazu Uncle and I were all working
together, to gather information about the
whereabouts of all the local freedom fighters. The
number of freedom fighters in our area was
increasing daily. We used to arrange for meals and
shelter for them. Generally, they would not come
outside during the day. They would hide here and
there in some houses in the local villages.
Discussions regarding guerrilla operations took
place at night. Sometimes the operations were
conducted late at night. When the freedom fighters'
operations were conducted during the day,
repression from the Pakistan Army and the
Razakars would be stepped up: They would enter
the villages and search for "the Liberators". If they
couldn't find them, they would label a few other
people as "suspects," capture them, and take them
to the army camps. The Razakars would inflict
even crueler torture than the soldiers. Every day we
heard news about their cruelty. And they didn't just

torture the freedom fighters; they would also rape the local young women, especially if they were Hindu women who had not fled to India. Married women were not safe either.

One notorious Razakar, whose name was Khilafat, lived in the nearby village of Sandiara. He was known to actually carry out the torture of young boys, ruthlessly, right in his own house. His presence made all the residents of Sandiara, and its neighboring villages, very uneasy. He would actually carry out the torture of young boys, ruthlessly, right in his own house. Khilafat was seen as a devil. He handed many people over to the Pakistan Army.

Khilafat ruled his village by terror. Every day, his Razakar group would abduct some villagers as part of their hunt for "the Liberators". They forcibly seized chickens and goats from the villagers. If they found out that somebody had gone to India from a particular house, they did their worst to the people remaining in that house. And Khilafat's house became known as a torture chamber.

The freedom fighters targeted the Razakar leader Khilafat, who was an ally of the Pakistan Army. They made a plan to kill him. One night, the noise of a bomb blast resounded from a distance, along with the sound of a Sten submachine gun firing. We had been asleep. Waking up and hearing all these noises of war, I began to think that the army had attacked somewhere nearby, and to wonder if we should now escape from the village.

But the shooting noises stopped after a while. Then there was silence. Khilafat, the Razakar, was killed the next morning. After the villagers heard about this, crowds of them rushed to Khilafat's house jubilantly. Thousands of people were crossing the canal to get to the house. The canal ran by Khilafat's house. What excitement, what joy the people (including me) experienced that day! Two or three of us from my house ran over to his house, and found that no living person was inside it. All of his captives had escaped. Khilafat had been hanged. People were shouting curses at his body, in rage. Some people threw their shoes at it. Some started kicking the dead body with their feet. The people's rage was so extreme, that they didn't even spare the dead body. I wondered if this was what this man deserved? What a ruthless reaction to his crimes! One villager started yelling loudly, like a madman, in filthy language, about Khilafat, telling us, "My brother was a freedom fighter. This Khilafat tortured him ruthlessly. He used to claim that Pakistan could not be broken by people trained in India, and that the Pakistani soldiers were the descendants of kings, so nobody would be able to defeat them. Now, see what has happened!"

The Razakars had wielded a hammer against this man's brother, the freedom fighter, injuring both of his hands, so that he could not hold a gun. He died not long afterwards. He had been living two or three miles away from our village.

At the end of October, Father had returned to our village from Dhaka. Ranga Uncle did not leave the village again. Happy days had now come to our family. Our house was full, and joyous, again, and our family content. Our morale and optimism had risen greatly. I no longer felt alone, having a full family around me now. There was peace in my mind. We heard from Father that the Freedom Fighters had already successfully staged a few operations in Dhaka. The guerilla war had now started. Meanwhile, we were also hearing, on the radio, from All India Radio-Kolkata, the BBC, and the Provisional Government's Independent Bangladesh Radio Station ("Swadhin Bangla Betar Kendra"), news of a series of attacks conducted by freedom fighters in different areas. This was exciting! We loved being able to get the latest news from the radio now. The news programs on the BBC, All India Radio-Kolkata, and Swadhin Bangla Betar Kendra were now conveying much cheering news to us. We would be especially enthralled when listening to the programs of the Independent Bangladesh Radio Station. These were ecstatic, hope-bolstering experiences. M.K. Akhtar Mukul's humorous program, "the Extreme Letter," always raised laughter among us. Broadcast talks about the various aspects of the war from Professor Abul Ahsan, at whose house we had stayed for a night, in the village of Alokdia in Magura, also encouraged us immensely. And, in the evenings, the station would play the songs of Abdul Jabbar and Apel Mahmud, which we would always listen to before going to sleep.

Every day on the news there were reports about freedom fighters destroying culverts and bridges.

The Razakars became terrified, and the Pakistani soldiers too. But the Razakars did not leave the army camp. The Pakistan Army was busy with trying to reorganize itself. One afternoon, in the middle of November, we heard the sounds of bomb blasts, from a distance. Everyone was murmuring that the bombs were being fired from field cannons in the border region. We would hear the sounds of bombing every day. Trained freedom fighters continued to return from India. One of the four young guys that I had spent time with, on a regular basis, in the village, (we called him Abid Uncle), now returned home, having finished his training. This further increased our optimism.

CHAPTER 11: **DECEMBER**

Since November, there had been continuous bombing along the border. The sounds of bombing were heard every day. There was tremendous tension along the border. The freedom fighters were staging attacks here and there. In some places, face to face battles took place. Highly irritated and frustrated, the Pakistan Army launched an air strike near Agra, on India's western front with Pakistan, on 3rd December. That evening, Prime Minister Indira Gandhi made an address on Indian Radio, declaring war against Pakistan. On December 4th, I saw, in the sky, an Indian airplane rushing towards Dhaka at enormous velocity, at around 10 am. The war was really on now. That night, we heard on the radio news that all the "Sabre Jets" (fighter planes) that Pakistan had had in East Pakistan had been destroyed. The next day, the Pakistani soldiers who'd been based at the cantonment garrison of Jessore fled from it. With the fall of Jessore, Pakistani control over Jhenaidah town also collapsed. That night, the news reported that Jessore and Jhenaidah were both free. My blood was boiling with excitement. I had become confident that the country would eventually be completely free. Now, all of us were just waiting to see when this would happen.

The morning after I heard that news, I got on my bike and set off in the direction of Jhenaidah and Jessore. When I reached the Kumar River, and could see, across it, the electric wires along the roads of Jhenaidah city, my heart started dancing. How long had it been since I'd last seen the city? After crossing the river on the ferry, I rode the bike for seven miles along the C & B Road. The streets were nearly empty, with no army vehicles coming through to frighten people. When I reached the city center at around 12 noon, I saw a city recovering its spirit, with many people spontaneously embracing each other. I saw a large number of Indian artillery vehicles proceeding towards Dhaka, carrying field cannons. Local people were climbing up on the Indian military tanks, and they were kissing and embracing the Indian soldiers, even bringing them sugar cane. What joy! Pakistan, trying to maintain its "unity," and domination over Bengalis, had tortured, plundered, and killed people in the name of religion. But now, the people of Bengal were going to defeat them, with the help of Indian soldiers.

I looked for my aunt and uncle in Jhenaidah, but did not find them. So, in the afternoon, I returned to our family's house in the village. The villagers wanted to know about Jhenaidah. I briefly summarized for them what I had seen and learned when I was there.

As the day passed, the Joint Force (the Indian Army together with Bengali freedom fighters) was moving forward towards Dhaka. Soldiers coming from all over the country were now encircling Dhaka. There were also paratroopers parachuting down to join their fellow soldiers in the area. General Manekshaw, the Indian Army chief, began regularly addressing Pakistani troops by radio broadcast, recommending that they surrender to the Joint Force, and assuring them that they would receive honorable treatment from the Indian troops if they did so. Bombs were falling from the sky, dropped by MIG fighter planes. The Joint Force was focusing its initial efforts on gaining control of Dhaka, and was rapidly accomplishing this goal.

We heard on the radio that Pakistan had put pressure on the United Nations to force India to cease its actions in East Pakistan/ Bangladesh. We knew that the Pakistani regime's control over our Bangladesh would survive if the Security Council passed a pro-Pakistan resolution that had been proposed to it. If that happened, then all our efforts, the freedom struggle of Bengalis, would have been for nothing. But, the next day, we heard that the Soviet Union, using its veto power, had shattered the hopes of the Pakistani regime for such support. Nevertheless, Pakistan continued to try to hold on to its distant Eastern wing by any means necessary.

Despite its all-out efforts to maintain its control over East Pakistan, the Pakistani regime was now doomed to lose that control. It was essentially isolated from the international community, and had no alternative but to surrender. On December 15, we learned that the Pakistan Army had, indeed, agreed to surrender. The surrender agreement would be signed on the Racecourse ground. With the Pakistani surrender of December 16, the nine-month-long bloody war finally ended.

I was in the village on that day. Everyone looked happy, their eyes were full of joy. I had thought that after getting their freedom, the villagers would erupt in joy - there would be fireworks, the drums would be beaten, and there would be dancing all around. But none of this happened. The intense war had left the people too exhausted to immediately express their happiness fully.

Outwardly, they seemed almost unchanged. But this was natural, not a cause for concern. There was no more fear now, no more anticipation of tragedy. The people were at peace in their minds now. On the day when Pakistan lost control of Dhaka, on the day of that victory, my father's younger brother, MNA Uncle, came to the village in a jeep. Alighting at home, he hugged my father. This was their first meeting since MNA Uncle's departure from Dhaka in March. The mother of the Razakar from our village then came over to our house, and knelt down and clutched my uncle's ankles, in a gesture of respect, and perhaps a plea for forgiveness. Someone standing nearby told us that her son was a Razakar. MNA Uncle pushed her hands off his legs, and then set off for Katalagari. After giving a brief post-liberation speech at a gathering there, he left the country again, for Kolkata.

Two to three days after Bangladesh's independence was achieved, the local villagers, together with the freedom fighters, proceeded to occupy the Sailkupa camp. The Pakistani soldiers had already escaped from it, leaving the Razakars defenseless. The people were bursting with rage against the Razakars. It seemed that if they could grab hold of some of the Razakars, they would grind them to a pulp. The Razakars had inflicted so much torture on the people, that now that they'd become powerless, they were surely doomed to suffer terrible consequences. During the night, some of the local villagers, together with some freedom fighters, surrounded the army camp. The operation started in the morning. Two or three grenades were detonated. There was shooting, which continued for some time. Some of the Razakars in the camp loudly cried out, "Brothers! Please let us be! Do not kill us! We will surrender."

After a while, the Razakars all came out of the camp, one by one, holding their hands up. They were wore brown shirts and lungis. All of them were told to stand in front of the green field adjacent to the camp. Twenty to twenty-five Razakars obediently went to stand there, in a row. The Razakar from our village was also there. Many of the local people gathered around to watch this event. At one point, these villagers, in their rage, tried to shove some of the Razakars down to the ground; but they failed in these attempts, and so began to aim kicks at the standing men – at both their legs and their mid-sections. This continued for some time. Eventually, the Razakars were sent back into the camp. Many people asked angrily, "Why are they being allowed to go on living?" The Razakars would not have let villagers go, after getting a hold of them. I also did not understand why they were allowed to live. I thought we needed to be crueler to them, after all the terrible torture they had inflicted. Later, Indian soldiers came and took the Razakars somewhere else; they were not left in our hands.

Our country was now independent. We could have dreams for the future now, and new lives. My family was joyfully obsessed with the idea of returning to Dhaka. Some of the villagers told us, "Yes, go to Dhaka and rent a big house. We will come and stay in your house. We will see what the capital of the independent Bangladesh looks like. We won't forget you. Will you remember the village? Will you remember us?"

The final words stuck my mind. Really, I wondered, if we go back to the city, will we be able to see them again? Will we come back to the village again? I smiled softly and told them, "With your help, we were able to find refuge here."

Loving a place, a home, deeply, never prevents anyone from returning to it, and it did not do so with us.

At noontime that day, as I rested on the bed on the east side of the house, the villagers' final words flashed through my mind: "Will you remember the village? Will you remember us?" I heard the sweet sound of birds calling from a distant place. The fir tree caught my eyes through the window. The birds flew about in the sunny sky. I reflected on our eight-month stay in the village. For urban people, returning to their city from the harder life of this village would not be expected to be difficult. So, why was the thought of going back there causing me pain today? This village had given us shelter in our times of crisis, in difficult times. Its trees, ponds, and walkways, its environment, and its people were now a real home to me. I had not realized what a large space in my heart it had come to occupy. Now, when I thought of abandoning the village, I felt as if it would cause me to lose myself. There is great sadness in farewell. There would come a time when this village and its people would be only a blur in my mind, as would be blurred the troubles, pains and sorrow, we had suffered in the recent months. Perhaps this is a normal and natural phenomenon.

When Pakistan had been going all out to retain its power over East Pakistan, when the prospects for breaking the shackles of Pakistani rule had seemed most bleak -- at that time, Bangladesh had been born, thanks to the sacrifices of the freedom fighters. Then, a new era emerged. The echoes of the unfinished stories of the last nine months, filled with sadness, were still all around us, but Bangladesh had now awakened. Delight and joy were now everywhere, in the new Bangladesh. Bengalis were having new hopes, new plans, and new thoughts about the future of the country.

However, although the country was now independent, not all of those who had gone off to India had returned yet. Everyone in the country was waiting to be reunited with their dear ones. My mother still wept. My younger brother had not come back home. Even though the country had become independent on 16th December, our victory could not be complete without the return of my younger brother.

Father was now in the village. He had almost been ready to return to Dhaka, but then he did not go. Perhaps, in his heart, there was still too strong a desire to see my younger brother, to allow him to leave this place.

On one winter morning, I again set off to Jhenaidah city on my bike. As I was cycling along, I wondered if those who'd gone to India might all have returned by now. After completing the sixteen-mile journey, I saw that the shops were open in Jhenaidah. The atmosphere of the city center was still joyous. Things were back to normal here. The homes of two of my uncles were in this city, but they had both gone off to India. But maybe they were back now? The house of my father's immediate elder brother was located at the eastern end of the city. He had lived in Jhenaidah city for many years. During the war, he had gone to India, leaving the house unprotected. I went to check it. He was not there, and neither was my aunt, his wife. I opened the wooden gate of the house, and went into the yard. I saw a young boy sitting on a chair, on the veranda on the south side of the house, looking in front of him. When my bicycle's bell rang, he looked my way. It was my younger brother sitting there! He was wearing a brown shirt and yellow shoes. I was dumbfounded. For a while I kept looking at him, speechless. And he looked at me. We were both mum for some time. Then I approached him and, when I got close, embraced him, and said, "Let's go home!"

He sat on the handlebars of my bike. I pedaled us all the way back to the village home, though the fifteen-mile journey was tough. We reached home at about noon, and then neighbors came by and filled up our courtyard. Everyone was looking at my younger brother. My mother, father, sisters, and little brother stood on the verandah of the house. Nobody's eyes looked wet. All the pent-up, painful emotions could not be allowed to start coming out now, or there would be terrible outbursts of crying. My younger brother now had a big crowd of people around him. Raihan Uncle, the freedom fighter from our village, walked up to him, carrying an SLR gun. My younger brother took the gun from him and fired it up into the sky. This frightened some of the people around him a bit, and they backed away a little. But the shooting of the SLR gun was like the raising of a flag of victory. This fifteen-year-old freedom fighter had returned home from the war. Joy was erupting over the earth.